THE LIFE AND JOURNEY OF ENAVED & NAVA

WRITTEN BY **THOMAS DEVANE**

ILLUSTRATED BY **DEANDRA ROY**

This book belongs to:

....

"Daddy, what does I love you mean? I always hear you say," I love you to me, Nava and Mommy."

"EnaVed, that's a great question and I'm happy to explain it,"

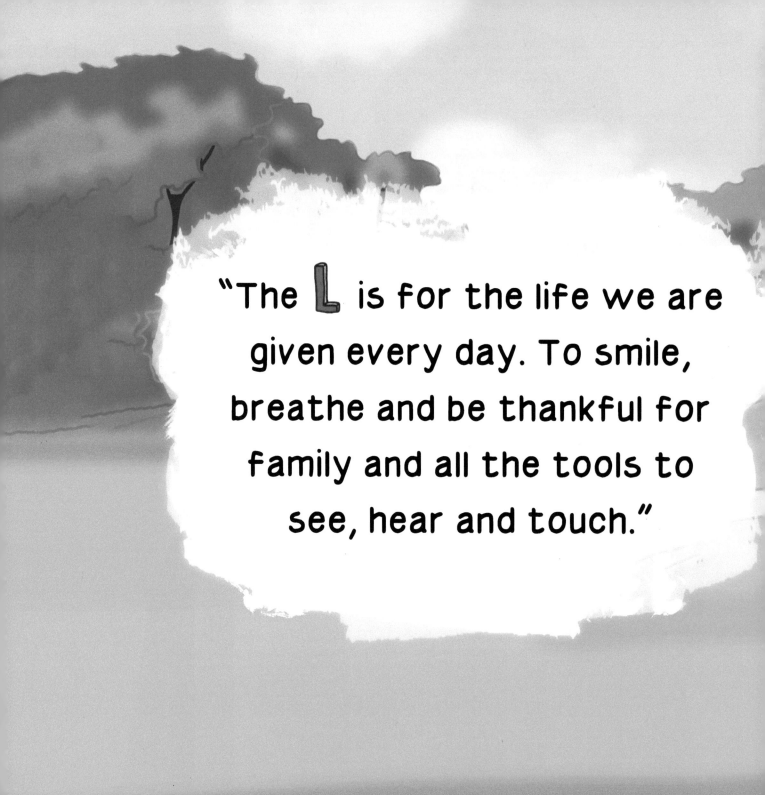

"The **L** is for the life we are given every day. To smile, breathe and be thankful for family and all the tools to see, hear and touch."

"The **O** is for being objective in our day to day world so that we can be fair to one another." Being fair to you, Nava, Mommy and I, allows us to enjoy one another's spirit.

"The **V** is for the voice we are given from the high and mighty above. It allows us to express ourselves and to let our family know all about our good days and our not so good days. We use our voices to advocate for ourselves to ensure we are treated fairly an equally."

"The E is for everything I enjoy about you, Nava and your mother."

"The eternity of my life's commitment, is to voice my feelings for you all and to let you know how much I enjoy being your father and your mother's husband."

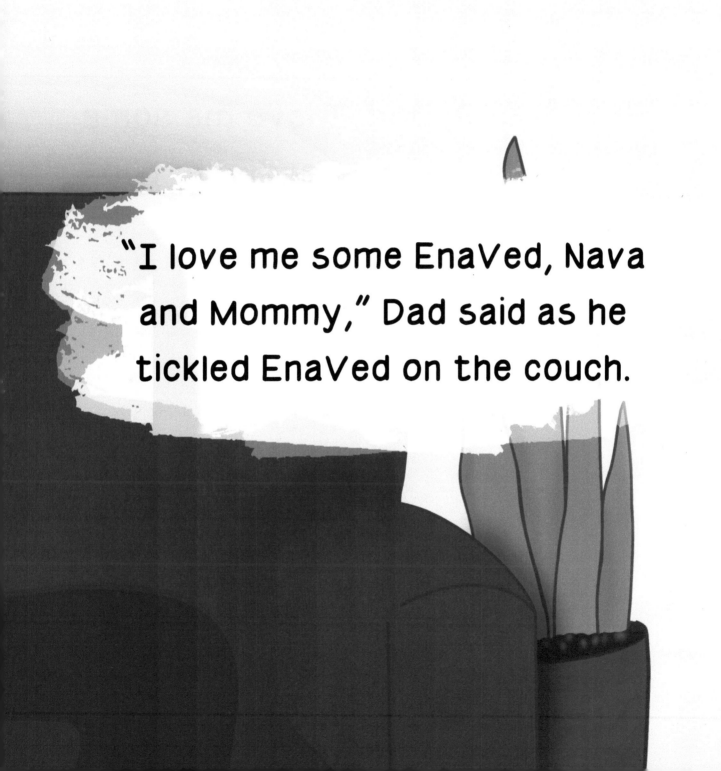

"I love me some EnaVed, Nava and Mommy," Dad said as he tickled EnaVed on the couch.

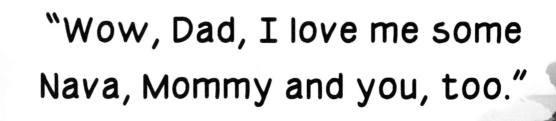

"Wow, Dad, I love me some Nava, Mommy and you, too."

CPSIA information can be obtained
at www.ICGtesting.com
Printed in the USA
LVHW050309100921
697443LV00011B/482